Based on the best-selling book by Doug Fields

Participant's Guide

PURPOSE DRIVEN®
YOUTH
MINISTRY

Training Kit

ZondervanPublishingHouse

Grand Rapids, Michigan
A Division of HarperCollinsPublishers

Purpose-Driven Youth Ministry Training Kit Participant's Guide

Copyright © 2000 by Doug Fields

Requests for information should be addressed to:

ZondervanPublishingHouse
Grand Rapids, Michigan 49530

ISBN: 0-310-23109-4

Interior design by designpointinc.com

Printed in the United States of America

00 01 02 03 04 05 /DC/ 10 9 8 7 6 5 4 3 2

CONTENTS

WELCOME TO PURPOSE-DRIVEN YOUTH MINISTRY TRAINING!

Someone in your church believes you're an important asset to your youth ministry—which is why this workbook is in your hands. Congratulations for being a leader who plays an important role on your youth ministry team, whether up front or behind the scenes. Whether you're an adult leader or a student leader, you have strengths to contribute.

It's amazing how many youth ministries plod along from school year to school year, scheduling program after program, teaching lesson after lesson—all without knowing why they're doing what they're doing. The reasons for this are many. Sometimes youth workers just don't think about the whys of their ministry. Other times youth leaders are dropped into programs with lots of deadlines or lots of crises, and they simply don't have time to ponder the whys. Some youth workers are slaves to tradition, consciously or unconsciously.

On the other hand, being a slave isn't bad as long as you're a slave to the right things. The point of Purpose Driven Youth Ministry is, frankly, to make your youth ministry a slave to biblical purposes instead of to programs—and all in order to win students to Christ and help them grow in their faith.

Like you, I'm a youth worker who works in the real world of youth ministry—where no program is perfect, no response is what I expected, and no generalization is without exception. So be assured that this Purpose-Driven stuff is tried and tested through successes and failures. The Purpose-Driven strategy doesn't emerge from an ivory tower or a think tank, but from a real-life youth ministry in a real-life church, filled with real students, volunteers, and parents.

It is my desire that your students grow in their intimacy with Jesus Christ, and I firmly believe that the Purpose-Driven Youth Ministry strategy will help you move them in that direction. I hope it will challenge you, ruffle a few feathers, and clarify your thinking and youth ministry practice.

Enjoy the process!

—Doug Fields

THE YOUTH LEADER'S SPIRITUAL LIFE

How is your heart?

In this session you will—

- Analyze why dependence on God's power is the foundation for a healthy youth ministry.
- Compare and contrast being a person of God with doing the work of God.
- Evaluate the condition of your heart.

Discovery
BUILDING A HEALTHY YOUTH MINISTRY

Zeal without knowledge is not good; a person who moves too quickly may go the wrong way.
Proverbs 19:2 NLT

1. Building a healthy youth ministry

_____ . It doesn't happen

_____ .

If the ax is dull and its edge unsharpened, more strength is needed but skill will bring success.
Ecclesiastes 10:10

2. Building a healthy youth ministry takes

_____ . It needs more

than _____ and

_____ .

Each of us did the work the Lord gave us. The one who plants and the one who waters work as a team with the same purpose.
1 Corinthians 3:5, 8 NLT

3. Building a healthy youth ministry takes a

_____ that is willing to work

together. It isn't a _____ job.

The Lord is exalted, for he dwells on high; he will fill Zion with justice and righteousness. He will be the sure foundation for your times, a rich store of salvation and wisdom and knowledge; the fear of the Lord is the key to this treasure.

Isaiah 33:5-6

4. Building a healthy youth ministry takes leaders who

_____ on God's power. It isn't just

about _____ and

_____ .

Video
HOW IS YOUR HEART?

● Don't start with _____ or

_____ , but instead start with

_____ .

● Doing is _____

_____

_____

the way my heart is

**the way I'd like
my heart to be**

Reflection
SO WHAT'S YOUR HEART LIKE?

The most important quality for a leader in ministry is a pure heart—a heart the leader allows God to change, mold, and reshape according to his will.

Mark an X on each scale below to indicate the approximate condition of your heart.

satisfied	●————————●	dissatisfied
humble	●————————●	proud
encouraging	●————————●	critical
available	●————————●	too busy
empathetic	●————————●	uncaring

On the top heart, list other qualities that describe the condition of your heart. Include both strengths and weaknesses.

On the bottom heart, explain how you would like to change and how God might help you do those things.

When you're finished, spend a few minutes in silent prayer.

Include any of the following—

- Thank God for calling you to influence students.

- Ask God to help you see new truths about yourself.

- Discuss with God truths you've already realized about yourself.

- Ask God to help you change in the areas you've just written about.

- Thank God for his faithfulness and love.

- Renew your commitment to God and to the ministry he's called you to serve in.

Video
FIRST THINGS FIRST: GETTING YOUR HEART RIGHT

Take some time with _____,
some time _____, and some time
_____ .

Connection
DEPENDING ON GOD

1. When have you experienced relying on God to do something in ministry? When have you tried to do something in your own strength? Compare the two situations.

2. Why is dependence on God important for the leaders in our ministry? What will this bring to our ministry?

3. Why do you feel we are so susceptible to the path of *doing*? Why is it so easy to focus on actions?

4. Why is *being* so difficult to find? What roles do your church's values play? Do they help or hinder?

5. What do you feel is the greatest asset you bring to the ministry? Do you feel that this asset gets appreciated and affirmed? Give an example.

6. Would you consider your life busy? What three areas take up most of your time? How can a full schedule keep a person from focusing on being a person of God? What is the greatest barrier you face that keeps you from spending time with God?

On the other hand...

- What does it even mean to *rely on God* or to *depend on God?* Depend on him for exactly what? For what sorts of things?

- What does it look like to rely on God in your office...in the field...in class...in your car...with your friends, spouse or kids...or in other primary relationships?

Discovery
WAYS TO INCREASE YOUR DEPENDENCE ON GOD

I know your deeds, your hard work and your perseverance... You have persevered and have endured hardships for my name, and have not grown weary. Yet I hold this against you: You have forsaken your first love. Remember the height from which you have fallen! Repent and do the things you did at first.
Revelation 2:2-5

Draw close to God, and God will draw close to you.
James 4:8 NLT

1. Take _____ for the condition of your heart.

Search me, O God, and know my heart; test me and know my thoughts. Point out anything in me that offends you, and lead me along the path of everlasting life.
Psalm 139:23-24 NLT

The crucible for silver and the furnace for gold, but the Lord tests the heart.   Proverbs 17:3

Trust in the Lord with all your heart; do not depend on your own under-standing. Seek his will in all you do, and he will direct your paths.
Proverbs 3:5-6, NLT

2. Find time for occasional _____
_____.

"My grace is sufficient for you, for my power is made perfect in weakness." Therefore I will boast all the more gladly about my weaknesses, so that Christ's power may rest on me.
2 Corinthians 12:9

We have this treasure in jars of clay to show that this all-surpassing power is from God and not from us.
2 Corinthians 4:7

We loved you so much that we were delighted to share with you not only the gospel of God but our lives as well, because you had become so dear to us.
1 Thessalonians 2:8

3. Realize that God wants to _____

_____ .

4. Rejoice that you get a chance to

_____ in others.

On the other hand...

- A "heart check" apparently has something to do with searching, testing, seeking. How do you picture giving yourself a regular "heart check"?

- Your life—and particularly your spiritual growth—has undoubtedly been influenced by someone special or at least memorable. Who was it? Do you sense that God somehow used this person? How did this person invest in you? How were you affected?

- What does it mean to share your life with someone? Does it mean the same thing to share yourself? Your experiences? Your hopes, struggles, successes, failures, doubts, fears?

- Finish this sentence: Sharing my life with my students means that I will let them see—

- *God, I'll do whatever it takes to get my heart right so that I depend on your power.* What does it mean "to get my heart right"? Does it mean you have to be perfect? Does it have something to do with your motives? Your desire for God?

Making It Personal

I pray also that the eyes of your heart may be enlightened in order that you may know the hope to which he has called you, the riches of his glorious inheritance in the saints, and his incomparably great power for us who believe. That power is like the working of his mighty strength, which he exerted in Christ when he raised him from the dead and seated him at his right hand in the heavenly realms, far above all rule and authority, power and dominion, and every title that can be given, not only in the present age but also in the one to come.
Ephesians 1:18-21

1. Since the power that raised Jesus from the dead is available to you as a believer, describe how you see God's power working in your life.

Test me, O Lord, and try me, examine my heart and my mind.
Psalm 26:2

2. A while ago, you spent some time evaluating the condition of your heart. Which of those areas do you struggle in the most? Next to each area, write down the name of a friend who might help you grow in that area of your life and hold you accountable.

3. What element of the youth ministry, if anything, fuels your struggles?

Destruction is certain for those who look to Egypt for help, trusting their cavalry and chariots instead of looking to the Lord, the Holy One of Israel.
Isaiah 31:1 NLT

Trust In the Lord with all your heart and lean not on your own understanding.
Proverbs 3:5

4. What conditions make it difficult for you to rely on God's power? What can you do to change the conditions or your thinking about the conditions?

But [God] said to me, "My grace is sufficient for you, for my power is made perfect in weakness." Therefore I will boast all the more gladly about my weaknesses, so that Christ's power may rest on me. That is why, for Christ's sake, I delight in weaknesses, in insults, in hardships, in persecutions, in difficulties. For when I am weak, then I am strong.
2 Corinthians 12:9-10

5. List three weaknesses you have as a youth worker that you need God's power to overcome.

6. How do you usually compensate for your personal weaknesses? Are you more likely to rely on God's power or your own?

7. Describe the last time you felt God's power working through you.

8. What are some practical ways you might rely on God's power in your ministry?

But we have this treasure in jars of clay to show that this all-surpassing power is from God and not from us. We are hard pressed on every side, but not crushed; perplexed, but not in despair; persecuted, but not abandoned; struck down, but not destroyed. We always carry around in our body the death of Jesus, so that the life of Jesus may also be revealed in our body.
2 Corinthians 4:7-10

9. What have been some of your greatest frustrations or struggles in ministry recently?

10. What possible reasons are there for God allowing these experiences?

11. How have you seen his power displayed to others?

His divine power has given us
everything we need for life and
godliness through our knowledge
of him who called us by his own
glory and goodness.
2 Peter 1:3

12. Are you beginning to feel desparate about needing God's power to show up in your life and ministry? In what situation?

When the people of Israel saw
the mighty power that the Lord
had displayed against the
Egyptians, they feared the Lord
and put their faith in him and his
servant Moses.
Exodus 14:31, NLT

13. Not only did the people put their faith in God, they also put their faith in Moses. What implications might this truth have for your ministry to students?

14. Name two students you hope will put their faith in God because of your leadership. Pray for them.

15. Write a letter to God and tell him your thoughts, ideas, feelings, and questions as a result of this training session.

On the other hand...

- Have you ever needed something badly, and asked God to show his power and help you—and nothing happened? How did God's silence affect you? What does Isaiah 55:8 say about God's silences: "For my thoughts are not your thoughts, neither are your ways my ways."

- If you don't feel God's power working through you, does that mean God's power isn't working through you? Why?

- Jesus displayed his power by *not* using it when he went to the cross. Can you think of time in your life when God showed himself in your weakness rather than your strength?

- Some Christians believe that to *be*, you have to *do*—do Bible reading, do prayer, do your devotions, do church, etc. Other Christians define *being* as paying attention to God, noticing God, listening to God. What do you think?

- How can you make sure you don't add to students' busyness in your youth group?

WHY YOUR MINISTRY EXISTS

5 biblical purposes for youth ministry

In this session you will—

* Investigate five biblical purposes for youth ministry.

* Apply the purposes to the context of your ministry.

* Identify which purpose is your personal passion.

Video

5 BIBLICAL PURPOSES FOR YOUTH MINISTRY

Jesus replied: " 'Love the Lord your God with all your heart and with all your soul and with all your mind.' This is the first and greatest commandment. And the second is like it: 'Love your neighbor as yourself.' All the Law and the Prophets hang on these two commandments."
Matthew 22:37-40

The Great Commandment

Therefore go and make disciples of all nations, baptizing them in the name of the Father and of the Son and of the Holy Spirit, and teaching them to obey everything I have commanded you. And surely I am with you always, to the very end of the age.
Matthew 28:19-20

The Great Commission

The Five Purposes

1. "Love the Lord your God with all your heart" is a call to

_____ .

2. "Love your neighbor as yourself" is a call to

_____ .

3. "Go and make disciples of all nations" is a call to

_____ .

4. "Baptizing them" (incorporating them into the body of
believers) is a call to _____ .

5. "Teaching them to obey" is a call to

_____ .

The key to a healthy youth ministry, then, lies in understanding
and maintaining a _____ of the five
biblical purposes expressed in your youth ministry.

Discovery
THE MEANING OF THE 5 BIBLICAL PURPOSES

Worship is _____ God's presence and
honoring him with our lifestyles.

Ministry is _____ God's love by meeting
the needs of others with love.

Evangelism is _____ the good news of
Jesus Christ with those who don't yet have a personal relationship
with him.

Fellowship is _____ God's people into a family where they can be known, cared for, held accountable, and encouraged.

Discipleship is _____ God's people with his truth.

On the other hand...

- Which of these purposes seem the easiest to you? The most encouraging? Why?

- Which of these purposes seems the most difficult or even a bit frightening to you? Why?

- These may be among the *central* purposes in ministry, but are they the only purposes? Would you add any other purposes? Do any of your purposes relate to the five listed here?

- Do you think your youth group must participate in *all* the purposes in order to be healthy? Why or why not?

Connection
EXPLORING THE PURPOSES

1. What does *worship* look like for our youth group? What are some different ways to express worship? What is one thing you feel keeps our students from living out this purpose in their lives?

2. What does *ministry* look like for our youth group? What are some different ways to express ministry? What is one thing you feel keeps our students from living out this purpose in their lives?

3. What does *evangelism* look like for our youth group? What are some different ways to express evangelism? What is one thing you feel keeps our students from living out this purpose in their lives?

4. What does *fellowship* look like for our youth group? What are some different ways to express fellowship? What is one thing you feel keeps our students from living out this purpose in their lives?

5. What does *discipleship* look like for our youth group? What are some different ways to express discipleship? What is one thing you feel keeps our students from living out this purpose in their lives?

If you break into small groups to discuss the questions, use the spaces below to capture some of the comments other small groups share with the whole group.

worship

ministry

evangelism

fellowship

discipleship

On the other hand...

- Which of these purposes describes your youth group's most urgent need?

- Prioritize these purposes based on the needs of your youth group.

A LOOK AT THE PURPOSES IN THE EARLY CHURCH

As a group, read through the passage and discuss which of God's purposes were being fulfilled by the early church. Make a list of your findings.

They devoted themselves to the apostles' teaching and to the fellowship, to the breaking of bread and to prayer. Everyone was filled with awe, and many wonders and miraculous signs were done by the apostles. All the believers were together and had everything in common. Selling their possessions and goods, they gave to anyone as he had need. Every day they continued to meet together in the temple courts. They broke bread in their homes and ate together with glad and sincere hearts, praising God and enjoying the favor of all the people. And the Lord added to their number daily those who were being saved.
Acts 2:42-47

PURPOSE	PHRASE

COMMUNICATING THE PURPOSES CLEARLY

Video
WHY BE PURPOSE DRIVEN?

- To clarify the _____ of the ministry.

- To minimize _____ within the ministry.

- To maximize _____ for the ministry.

Reflection
IDENTIFYING OUR PERSONAL PASSIONS

Which of the five biblical purposes—evangelism, worship, fellowship, discipleship, ministry—are you most passionate about and why?

Which purpose has God especially gifted you for?

Making It Personal

When citing, "Teacher, which is the greatest commandment in the Law?" Jesus replied: "'Love the Lord your God with all your heart and with all your soul and with all your mind.' This is the first and greatest commandment. And the second is like it: 'Love your neighbor as yourself.' All the Law and the Prophets hang on these two commandments."

Matthew 22:36-40

Then Jesus came to them and said, "All authority in heaven and on earth has been given to me. Therefore go and make disciples of all nations, baptizing them in the name of the Father and of the Son and of the Holy Spirit, and teaching them to obey everything I have commanded you. And surely I am with you always, to the very end of the age."

Matthew 28:18-20

1. The five biblical purposes aren't just for the corporate church. Ultimately they should be expressed in the lives of all believers. How are these purposes expressed in your life?

- **Worship** (celebrating God's presence and honoring him with our lifestyles)

- **Ministry** (demonstrating God's love by meeting the needs of others with love)

- **Evangelism** (communicating the good news of Jesus Christ with those who don't yet have a personal relationship with him)

- **Fellowship** (incorporating God's people into a family where they can be known, cared for, held accountable, and encouraged)

- **Discipleship** (educating God's people with his truth)

28   SESSION 2 WHY YOUR MINISTRY EXISTS

2. Make some specific goals for each biblical purpose in your life. For example, a goal for fellowship can be—I need to be known, so I will find a few other people and start a small group for Bible study, prayer, and accountability.

But thanks be to God, who always leads us in triumphal procession in Christ and through us spreads everywhere the fragrance of the knowledge of him. For we are to God the aroma of Christ among those who are being saved and those who are perishing.
2 Corinthians 2:14-15

3. Paraphrase this verse to make it meaningful to your own life.

On the other hand...

- In the spirit of the 2 Corinthians verse on this page, what are some practical ways students could notice your "soul fragrance"?

THE STUDENTS YOU CAN REACH

Targeting different audiences

In this session you will—

- Define target audience and establish the importance of identifying it.

- Evaluate the target audience of your youth ministry.

- Learn how to integrate target audience and biblical purpose to determine programming.

Video
TARGETING DIFFERENT AUDIENCES

1. One program can't effectively target

_____

or fulfill all five biblical _____ .

2. Different audiences exist, and identifying them will lead to a

_____ .

3. When you take time to identify your target audience, you can

- _____ programs with specific students in mind.

- Better _____ and

  _____ students' needs.

- Help your regular students know who to

  _____ to what programs.

Discovery
IDENTIFYING OUR TARGET AUDIENCE

1. We have _____ target audiences within our ministry.

2. The target audiences are defined by

_____ .

3. Each level of spiritual commitment (target audience) should be classified in terms people _____

_____ .

On the following scale, mark the point on the line that indicates how easy or difficult it seems to you to identify our target audience. Explain your feelings.

impossible   •————————————•   no problem

What are some benefits to identifying a target audience other than what we've talked about?

How can we appreciate where a student is on her spiritual journey while identifying her level of spiritual maturity?

What are some target audiences we're already aware of in our student ministry?

What spiritual commitments exist on our leadership team? How do these mirror the commitments in our students?

On the other hand...

- Is there something about trying to identify a student's level of spiritual maturity that makes you a bit uneasy? Why or why not?

- Are levels of spiritual commitment the same for leaders as for students? Just for fun, create your own list of spiritual commitments for your leadership team.

Connection

IDENTIFYING SPIRITUAL COMMITMENTS

As a group, discuss and list the major spiritual commitments a person could make. When you're done, number the list, beginning with the commitment you see as easiest and ending with the one you see as most difficult.

Video

5 LEVELS OF SPIRITUAL COMMITMENT

The community student has no _____ with Christ.

The crowd student is committed to _____ _____ Christ.

The congregation student is committed to a

_____ Christ and other Christians.

The committed student is committed to _____ in Christ through spiritual disciplines.

The core student is committed to _____ because of Christ and _____ him with others.

On the other hand...

- Based on what you know of your students and of your community—and in your own words—define the five levels of commitment. (For example: *Our community students are bored, hard to get involved, redneck, party on weekends, clueless about world events, unmotivated, and afraid of church.*)

Connection

CREATING TARGET AUDIENCE PROFILES

TARGET AUDIENCE PROFILE

Profile Groups	Spiritual Commitment What are these students committed to spiritually?	Spiritual Needs What do these students need to help them take the next step?	Programs What programs will help meet their needs?
Community student	no measurable spiritual commitment		
Crowd student	hearing about Christ		
Congregation student	a relationship with Christ and other Christians		
Committed student	growing in Christ through spiritual disciplines		
Core student	serving because of Christ and sharing him with others		

On the other hand...

- How can you be assured that a student is ready to grow spiritually—or even *wants* to grow?

- What markers could you use to determine whether a student wants to move into another level of commitment?

- What about when you believe a student is ready to go deeper, but the student doesn't want to? What, if anything, can you do?

Reflection
EVALUATING STUDENTS

Write the names of the students you have relationships with under the target audience they most closely fit. (You probably don't want to make public this exercise—especially since it's only a tool to help you gauge where your students are spiritually. Estimating another's spirituality is always tricky business.)

Target Audience	Students' Names
Community	
Crowd	
Congregation	
Committed	
Core	

On the other hand...

- Add one more C—*clueless*. Any students come to mind who you have no clue where they are spiritually? What can you do to find out where they are?

Reflection
EVALUATING OUR MINISTRY

Look at the big picture of our entire youth ministry. Using percentages, estimate how many kids are in each target audience.

MAIN STREET COMMUNITY CHURCH

Target Audience	Quantity/Percentage
Community*	1,600 students
Crowd	30%
Congregation	50%
Committed	15%
Core	5%
Total	100%

* The community is made up of all the students who live within a realistic driving distance from your church. Because they are not yet a part of your ministry, they shouldn't be assigned a percentage.

OUR MINISTRY

Target Audience	Quantity/Percentage
Community*	*(number of students)*
Crowd	
Congregation	
Committed	
Core	
Total	100%

I think our _____ is the healthiest target

audience in our ministry because—

* The community is made up of all the students who live within a realistic
driving distance from your church. Because they are not yet a part of your
ministry, they shouldn't be assigned a percentage.

On the other hand...

- Okay, now look at your youth group's students from some different perspectives—

churchy —— nonchurchy
urban —— suburban
mature —— immature
guys —— gals
charismatic —— noncharismatic
likable —— not likable
easy to work with —— difficult to work with
introverts —— extroverts

Organize your students according to these groupings—then compare *this* list with your chart of the 5 levels of commitment. Do you see any trends?

Discovery
BRINGING PURPOSE AND TARGET AUDIENCE TOGETHER TO DEVELOP PROGRAMS

To develop your programs, ask these three questions:

1. _____ do we want to attend this program primarily? *Who's our target audience?**

2. _____ primary biblical purpose do we want to fulfill? *What's our purpose?**

3. _____ will we do this? *How will we attract our target audience and meet our purpose?*

---

* Often more than one audience and purpose will be involved, but programs should *target* one.

Creating an effective program is the result of combining the *who* and *what* questions.

community + evangelism = New Year's Eve party
(who)　　　(what)　　　　　(how)

Our programs should _____ to reflect our changing target audience emphasis and our changing biblical purpose emphasis.

On the other hand...

- When you think about the *how* question, think creatively. Maybe your "program" (the *how*) focuses on relational youth ministry, for example, simply taking a student out for ice cream...or watching one of your girls play in her basketball game...or making your home available for kids to just come over and be with you. What else can you add to these programming ideas that aren't programs?

Making It Personal

For where your treasure is, there your heart will be also.
Luke 12:34

1. How do a person's commitments affect and determine the direction of his or her life?

And let us consider how we may spur one another on toward love and good deeds.
Hebrews 10:24

2. In your opinion, what's the best way to spur others toward love and good deeds?

3. Why do you think the author of Hebrews began this admonition with the word *consider*?

4. Why do people need customized encouragement?

Read John 4:1-42.

5. What kinds of barriers did Jesus break through to get to this woman? What steps did Jesus take to meet her where she was in her life?

6. How did reaching this woman possibly help Jesus reach the entire Samaritan community at Sychar?

While Jesus was having dinner at Matthew's house, many tax collectors and "sinners" came and ate with him and his disciples. When the Pharisees saw this, they asked his disciples, "Why does your teacher eat with tax collectors and "sinners"? On hearing this, Jesus said, "It is not the healthy who need a doctor, but the sick. But go and learn what this means: 'I desire mercy, not sacrifice.' For I have not come to call the righteous, but sinners."
Matthew 9:10-13

7. It's clear from this passage that tax collectors and sinners were comfortable with Jesus and religious people were not. What was it about Jesus that caused this?

8. How can you and your leadership team make "outsiders" comfortable?

To the weak I became weak, to win the weak. I have become all things to all men so that by all possible means I might save some.
1 Corinthians 9:22

9. What would an all-possible-means evangelistic approach look like in your ministry?

10. It's clear that Paul tried to accommodate everyone without compromising the gospel. (See Romans 1:16.) Why do you think accommodating is often criticized, especially by other believers?

11. What types of students do you naturally connect with (athletes, shy kids, computer nerds)? What types do you have a hard time connecting with?

And because of his words many more became believers.
John 4:41

The words of the wise bring healing.
Proverbs 12:18 NLT

12. When Jesus spoke to a particular person (or group of people), what kinds of things do you think he considered in order to best reach them with the truth?

For God so loved the world...
John 3:16

Jesus straightened up and asked her, "Woman, where are they? Has no one condemned you?" "No one, sir," she said. "Then neither do I condemn you," Jesus declared. "Go now and leave your life of sin."
John 8:10-11

13. What are some reasons it may be especially important to accept students for who they are?

14. Identify one fringe student in your ministry. Write a specific prayer about how you can best care for him or her.

On the other hand...

- List treasures that students in your group desire, along with the names of the students who want each of them. While you're at it, what are some of *your* treasures?

- That phrase from Hebrews 10 about "love and good deeds"...it sounds so—well, *religious*. What do those words mean to you in your day-to-day life?

- Write customized encouragements for three or four students in your group.

- The trouble with words like *consider* is that considering takes time. Okay, so go with that idea...think about taking the entire youth ministry leadership team away for a Day of Considering in silence and solitude. Unrealistic? Then what about a half day? Or an evening, or an hour of silence?

- List some barriers you have to break through in order to reach the kids in your youth group.

- Translate 1 Corinthians 9:22 into your own words, with specific examples of how to be like Paul. (For instance, if you want to reach a person who is grieving, you need to grieve with them.)

- It's clear from this 1 Corinthians verse that words are important. We know the Word of God has come to us in two ways: words he spoke through human authors (the Bible) and the living Word (Jesus). What influences you more—the words you hear from others or the words that are "spoken" through others' actions?

MATCHING THE RIGHT PURPOSE WITH THE RIGHT AUDIENCE

Developing programs with purpose

In this session you will—

- Examine general principles for fulfilling the five biblical purposes.

- List additional principles that will help you fulfill the five biblical purposes.

- Evaluate your youth ministry's programs.

Video
HOW TO FULFILL THE 5 BIBLICAL PURPOSES

EVANGELISM
You can fulfill the biblical purpose of evangelism by—

- Appreciating the _____ that evangelism brings to most students.

- Recognizing that evangelism is a _____ rather than a one-time program.

- Challenging your students with realistic _____.

On the other hand...

- *Evangelism is a process*—what does this statement mean? If a youth group with demographics similar to yours "did" evangelism continually, what would it look like? What are the key elements of such a program?

FELLOWSHIP

You can fulfill the biblical purpose of fellowship by—

- Beginning with the _____ question.

- Pursuing a strategy that includes _____

  on _____ .

- Setting a goal for your care plan to reflect the biblical

  "_____ ."

  ~ Love one another (John 13:34)

  ~ Serve one another (Galatians 5:13)

  ~ Accept one another (Romans 15:7)

  ~ Forgive one another (Colossians 3:13)

  ~ Greet one another (Romans 16:16)

  ~ Carry one another's burdens (Galatians 6:2)

  ~ Be devoted to one another (Romans 12:10)

  ~ Honor one another (Romans 12:10)

  ~ Instruct one another (Romans 15:14)

  ~ Submit to one another (Ephesians 5:21)

  ~ Encourage one another (1 Thessalonians 5:11)

We loved you so much that we were delighted to share with you not only the gospel of God but our lives as well, because you had become so dear to us.
1 Thessalonians 2:8

On the other hand...

- Read all those Bible verses on page 46—then describe a practical way to fulfill some of these commands in your youth ministry.

DISCIPLESHIP
You can fulfill the biblical purpose of discipleship by—

- Communicating the goal of discipleship as

  _____ ,

  not program attendance.

Therefore, my dear friends, as you have always obeyed—not only in my presence, but now much more in my absence—continue to work out your salvation with fear and trembling.
Philippians 2:12

- Introducing habits that will help students

  _____ .

- Pursuing _____ in your

  discipleship efforts.

On the other hand...

- What kinds of habits will help students grow on their own?

MINISTRY

You can fulfill the biblical purpose of ministry by—

- Providing ministry opportunities for

  _____ .

- Making your youth ministry's or your church's needs your

  _____ .

- Challenging everyone to _____ their

  unique SHAPE for ministry.

Spiritual gifts
Heart
Abilities
Personality
Experience

It was he who gave some to be
apostles, some to be prophets,
some to be evangelists, and
some to be pastors and teachers,
to prepare God's people for works
of service, so that the body of
Christ may be built up.
Ephesians 4:11-12

WORSHIP

You can fulfill the biblical purpose of worship by—

- Seeing worship is _____ than just

  singing.

  Worship is also expressed through—

  ~ prayer (Psalm 95:6)

  ~ hearing the Word (Deuteronomy 31:11)

  ~ giving (1 Corinthians 16:1-2)

  ~ baptizing (Romans 6:3-4)

  ~ meditating (Habakkuk 2:20)

  ~ taking the Lord's Supper (1 Corinthians 11:23-26)

I was glad when they said to me, "Let us go to the house of the Lord."
Psalm 122:1 NLT

And so, dear brothers and sisters, I plead with you to give your bodies to God. Let them be a living and holy sacrifice—the kind he will accept. When you think of what he has done for you, is this too much to ask?
Romans 12:1 NLT

They worshiped together at the Temple each day, met in homes for the Lord's Supper, and shared their meals with great joy and generosity—all the while praising God and enjoying the goodwill of all the people. And each day the Lord added to their group those who were being saved.
Acts 2:46-47 NLT

- Teaching worship as a celebration of God's presence reflected in our _____ .

- Realizing non-Christians can be _____ to by authentic Christian worship.

On the other hand...

- *Worship* is a fine word—but what does it mean? What would it look like if your lifestyle reflected your worship?

- Look at Romans 12:1-2 again. How does Paul define worship? What does it look like these days when one offers one's body as a living sacrifice?

Reflection
MY RESPONSE TO THE PRINCIPLES FOR FULFILLING THE BIBLICAL PURPOSES

Jot down your responses to the main points about each purpose presented in the last segment. Then choose one or two of the purposes you feel most passionate about, and list several principles to guide you in fulfilling each. (Avoid specific program ideas.)

EVANGELISM

My response

Additional principles

FELLOWSHIP

My response

Additional principles

DISCIPLESHIP

My response

Additional principles

MINISTRY

My response

Additional principles

WORSHIP

My response

Additional principles

Discovery

EVALUATING OUR YOUTH MINISTRY PROGRAMS

In the first column, list all the programs—formal and informal—
that your youth ministry offers. Answer the four questions for
each program in the remaining columns.

EVALUATING OUR YOUTH MINISTRY PROGRAMS

Program	Who is the primary target audience?	What is the primary biblical purpose?
1.		
2.		
3.		
4.		
5.		
6.		
7.		
8.		
9.		
10.		

How do the responsibilities of each adult leader fulfill the primary purpose and enhance the ministry to the target audience?	What is the next step for a student attending this program?

Connection
TAKING THE NEXT STEP

Video
CHANGE TAKES TIME!

- Evangelism, like the other four purposes, is not

  _____ . It's a

  _____ .

- Biblical purposes are not _____.
  What's new is how you apply them

  _____ —your own church and

  youth group.

Making It Personal

EVANGELISM

Therefore, if anyone is in Christ,
he is a new creation; the old has
gone, the new has come!
2 Corinthians 5:17

1. What practical differences do you detect between your Christian and non-Christian students? (Be honest—sometimes, to a youth leader's chagrin, the differences don't always put Christian students on the high moral road.)

2. What implications do these differences hold for your youth ministry's strategy for evangelism?

We proclaim him, admonishing
and teaching everyone with all
wisdom, so that we may present
everyone perfect in Christ.
Colossians 1:28

3. What types of students do you barely tolerate rather than enjoy?

4. *Evangelism is difficult if you don't like the natives you're called to reach.* Respond to this statement.

5. How can you help your students develop a heart for evangelism?

WORSHIP

You are my hiding place; you will protect me from trouble and surround me with songs of deliverance.
Psalm 32:7

Come, let us bow down in worship, let us kneel before the Lord our Maker; for he is our God and we are the people of his pasture, the flock under his care. Today, if you hear his voice, do not harden your hearts.
Psalm 95:6-8

6. In light of the Psalm 95 verses, why is worship important for students?

7. What if anything can you do to help students appreciate the importance of worship?

Remember that at that time you were separate from Christ, excluded from citizenship in Israel and foreigners to the covenants of the promise, without hope and without God in the world.
Ephesians 2:12

The thief comes only to steal and kill and destroy; I have come that they may have life, and have it to the full.
John 10:10

Therefore, since we are receiving a kingdom that cannot be shaken, let us be thankful, and so worship God acceptably with reverence and awe.
Hebrews 12:28

8. What do you feel is the relationship between *hope* and *worship?*

FELLOWSHIP

We loved you so much that we were delighted to share with you not only the gospel of God but our lives as well, because you had become so dear to us.
1 Thessalonians 2:8

9. In what practical ways can you share your life with students?

Let us not give up meeting together, as some are in the habit of doing, but let us encourage one another.
Hebrews 10:25

10. How do the students in your ministry benefit from your youth ministry meetings?

11. What kind of encouragement do the students in your youth ministry need?

12. What kind of encouragement do they receive?

13. Which of the "one anothers" listed below is most attractive to you and why?

~ Love one another (John 13:35)
~ Serve one another (Galatians 5:13)
~ Accept one another (Romans 15:7)
~ Forgive one another (Colossians 3:13)
~ Greet one another (Romans 16:16)
~ Bear one another's burdens (Galatians 6:2)
~ Be devoted to one another (Romans 12:10)
~ Honor one another (Romans 12:10)
~ Teach one another (Romans 15:14)
~ Submit to one another (Ephesians 5:21)
~ Encourage one another (1 Thessalonians 5:11)

14. In your own words, define *fellowship*.

DISCIPLESHIP

Preach the Word; be prepared in season and out of season; correct, rebuke and encourage—with great patience and careful instruction.
 2 Timothy 4:2

15. Compare the similarities of and contrast the differences between *correction*, *rebuke*, and *encouragement*.

16. Make a list of students you are most personally connected with. Identify whether the student most needs correction, rebuke, or encouragement. Describe how you will give them what they need.

17. What does it mean to be "prepared in season and out of season"?

Then we will no longer be infants, tossed back and forth by the waves, and blown here and there by every wind of teaching and by the cunning and craftiness of men in their deceitful scheming. Instead, speaking the truth in love, we will in all things grow up into him who is the Head, that is, Christ.
Ephesians 4:14-15

18. What are some false teachings that face your students and may possibly ensnare them? (For example, "Cheating is okay if you don't get caught," or "I'll be beautiful when I'm as thin as the girls in *Cosmopolitan*.")

It is not good to have zeal without knowledge, nor to be hasty and miss the way.
Proverbs 19:2

19. How does knowledge balance enthusiasm?

20. Why does Proverb 19:2 hold particular importance for students?

MINISTRY

Read Luke 10:30-35

21. What could you do to help your students become more like the Samaritan?

22. What would it take to get students aware of the needs of others and looking upon them with compassion?

23. Where do students see your examples of compassion?

**See, he is puffed up; his desires
are not upright—but the righteous
will live by his faith.**
Habakkuk 2:4

24. How can pride stand in the way of serving in ministry?

25. What is the best way to reduce pride in yourself and in the students you are connected to?

GROWING TOGETHER
Building a healthy team

In this session you will—

• Define healthy leadership team qualities.

• Evaluate your youth ministry's values.

• List principles of relational youth ministry.

Discovery
TRANSFORMING LEADERS INTO A TEAM

Two people can accomplish more than twice as much as one; they get a better return for their labor.
Ecclesiastes 4:9 NLT

The one who plans and the one who waters work as a team with the same purpose.
1 Corinthians 3:8 NLT

1. Players need to _____ on the power of God.

2. Players need to understand and _____ the direction of the youth ministry.

3. Players need to hold the same _____ for the youth ministry

4. Players need to minister within the context of _____ .

5. Players need to _____ one another.

For Discussion

● What elements or aspects of our team are functioning well?

● What factors have contributed to this health?

● What elements or aspects of our team do we need to work on?

● Is this team a good match for you? Do you feel safe ministering here? (You may not feel comfortable writing down any answer but a glowing one, but at least ask yourself the question—then act according to your silent answer.)

On the other hand...

- What if anything about those questions on page 64 seems overwhelming? Encouraging?

- If your team consists of *merely you and another person*, which of the overwhelming or encouraging items you listed above is most significant?

- If you have a team of *three or more*, which of the overwhelming or encouraging items you listed above is most significant?

Video
PRINCIPLES ARE ETERNAL, BUT VALUES CHANGE

- Values are descriptive words that communicate the

  _____ ,

  _____ , and

  _____ that should be reflected

  throughout the entire youth ministry.

- On one hand, God's _____ for

  youth ministry (worship, ministry, evangelism, fellowship,

  discipleship) originate in the Word—they are eternal,

  universal, unchanging, and they apply to the global church.

- On the other hand, your youth group's

  _____ originate with you, they

  change whenever you want to change them, and they apply

  specifically to your own youth group.

Discovery

DISCOVERING OUR VALUES

Connection

ASSESSING OUR VALUES

1. Judging from how our youth ministry is currently operating, what are the apparent values of our youth ministry?

2. Which of these values are worth keeping, in your opinion? Which of these values should be jettisoned?

3. What values, if any, are not reflected in our youth ministry, but you would like them to be?

Video
HOW TO BE A RELATIONAL YOUTH LEADER

1. Do whatever it takes to _____ .

2. Accept students for _____ .

3. Be honest about _____ .

4. Commit to being a _____
   factor in students' lives.

5. Pursue a _____ attitude.

6. Spend time with students _____ .

7. Remember that _____
   things are _____ things.

On the other hand...

- Which of these guidelines is most difficult for you to actually do? What makes it difficult for you?

Discovery
LOVING ONE ANOTHER

1. Keep _____
   with one another, confronting in a manner that's consistent
   with the Bible (with grace and truth).

2. Serve one another without _____ .

> Now, dear brothers and sisters, I appeal to you by the authority of the Lord Jesus Christ to stop arguing among yourselves. Let there be real harmony so there won't be divisions in the church. I plead with you to be of one mind, united in thought and purpose.
> 1 Corinthians 1:10 NLT

3. Support one another's _____ .

4. Be on the lookout for _____

to add to your team.

5. _____ together.

> They devoted themselves to the apostles' teaching and to the fellowship, to the breaking of bread and to prayer... Every day they continued to meet together in the temple courts. They broke bread in their homes and ate together with glad and sincere hearts, praising God and enjoying the favor of all the people. And the Lord added to their number daily those who were being saved.
> Acts 2:42, 46-47

On the other hand...

- Which of these guidelines is most difficult for you to actually do? What makes it difficult for you?

Making It Personal

> A new command I give you: Love one another. As I have loved you, so you must love one another. By this all men will know that you are my disciples, if you love one another.
> John 13:34-35

1. How can loving other leaders on your team affect the students in your ministry?

Read Acts 6:1-4, 7.

2. *Loving other leaders may be just as important as loving students.* Do you agree or disagree? Explain.

3. It's clear that two important tasks within the early church— the ministry of the Word and the distribution of food—were both suffering because the 12 disciples were trying to do too much. How does the too-few-doing-too-much phenomenon relate to your youth ministry?

4. What is your strongest contribution to your youth ministry?

We who are strong ought to bear with the failings of the weak and not to please ourselves... May the God who gives endurance and encouragement give you a spirit of unity among yourselves as you follow Christ Jesus, so that with one heart and mouth you may glorify the God and Father of our Lord Jesus Christ. Accept one another, then, just as Christ accepted you, in order to bring praise to God.
Romans 15:1, 5-7

5. What attitudes can poison unity?

6. How would other leaders on your team describe your attitude?

I appeal to you, brothers, in the name of our Lord Jesus Christ, that all of you agree with one another so that there may be no divisions among you and that you may be perfectly united in mind and thought... There should be no division in the body, but that its parts should have equal concern for each other.
1 Corinthians 1:10; 12:25

Be careful, however, that the exercise of your freedom does not become a stumbling block to the weak. For if anyone with a weak conscience sees you who have this knowledge eating in an idol's temple, won't he be emboldened to eat what has been sacrificed to idols? So this weak brother, for whom Christ died, is destroyed by your knowledge.
1 Corinthians 8:9-11

7. How does division among the leadership team negatively affect students? Is there division on your team that needs to be dealt with? How can you bring that about?

Starting a quarrel is like breaching a dam; so drop the matter before a dispute breaks out.
Proverbs 17:14

A gentle answer turns away wrath, but a harsh word stirs up anger.
Proverbs 15:1

An offended brother is more unyielding than a fortified city, and disputes are like the barred gates of a citadel.
Proverbs 18:19

8. Confrontation is a necessary part of life because we are make mistakes and get our feelings hurt. What are some biblical guidelines for confronting another leader?

But in fact God has arranged the parts in the body, every one of them, just as he wanted them to be.
1 Corinthians 12:18

Read Romans 12:3-8.

9. Are you are currently serving in the way you think God wants you to be serving? If not, what will it take for that to happen?

Therefore encourage one another and build each other up, just as in fact you are doing.
1 Thessalonians 5:11

10. What do you need to encourage you and keep you going?

11. How can you encourage some of the other leaders in your youth ministry?

On the other hand...

- Admit it—there's probably a leader on your team whom you certainly love in the spiritual sense, but whom you don't particularly like. So what do you do about it, if anything?

- It doesn't matter how small or large your youth group is—there always seems to be too much to do. What does this look like in your youth ministry? What can you stop doing? What *can't* you stop doing?

- Unfortunately, you can't always control the circumstances that affect your attitudes. And sometimes your feelings take a while to catch up to your actions. Bad-attitude days come to all of us—and they don't make appointments. How can you be a team player even when your attitude is below par?

- Even after you've determined your SHAPE and established your function in the youth ministry, you can be intimidated by people who are very good at what you're *not* good at. How can you avoid being intimidated by others' gifts? How can you become confident about your own place in ministry?

- Write yourself a letter from Jesus. Imagine he's writing to encourage you.

CONGRATULATIONS!

YOU'VE FINISHED PURPOSE-DRIVEN YOUTH MINISTRY TRAINING!

If you have any thoughts or questions about it, contact Doug Fields at www.dougfields.com

---

DOUG'S RESOURCES

For information on—

Purpose-Driven Youth Ministry seminars

The One-Minute Bible for Students

Bible Study curriculum

discipleship tools

volunteer training tapes

youth ministry internships at Saddleback Church

contact—

Making Young Lives Count

21612 Plano Trabuco Q-30

Trabuco Canyon, CA 92679

Phone: 949-830-4042

Fax: 949-830-4258

Resources can be viewed and ordered at
http://www.dougfields.com

PURPOSE
DRIVEN®
YOUTH
MINISTRY

PURPOSE
DRIVEN®
YOUTH
MINISTRY

NOTES

PURPOSE
DRIVEN®
YOUTH
MINISTRY

PURPOSE
DRIVEN®
YOUTH
MINISTRY

PURPOSE
DRIVEN®
YOUTH
MINISTRY

Resources from Youth Specialties

PROFESSIONAL RESOURCES

Administration, Publicity, & Fundraising (Ideas Library)
Developing Student Leaders
Equipped to Serve: Volunteer Youth Worker Training Course
Help! I'm a Junior High Youth Worker!
Help! I'm a Small-Group Leader!
Help! I'm a Sunday School Teacher!
Help! I'm a Volunteer Youth Worker!
How to Expand Your Youth Ministry
How to Speak to Youth...and Keep Them Awake at the Same Time
Junior High Ministry (Updated & Expanded)
The Ministry of Nurture: A Youth Worker's Guide to Discipling Teenagers
Purpose-Driven Youth Ministry
So That's Why I Keep Doing This! 52 Devotional Stories for Youth Workers
A Youth Ministry Crash Course
The Youth Worker's Handbook to Family Ministry

YOUTH MINISTRY PROGRAMMING

Camps, Retreats, Missions, & Service Ideas (Ideas Library)
Compassionate Kids: Practical Ways to Involve Your Students in Mission and Service
Creative Bible Lessons from the Old Testament
Creative Bible Lessons in 1 & 2 Corinthians
Creative Bible Lessons in John: Encounters with Jesus
Creative Bible Lessons in Romans: Faith on Fire!
Creative Bible Lessons on the Life of Christ
Creative Junior High Programs from A to Z, Vol. 1 (A-M)
Creative Junior High Programs from A to Z, Vol. 2 (N-Z)
Creative Meetings, Bible Lessons, & Worship Ideas (Ideas Library)
Crowd Breakers & Mixers (Ideas Library)
Downloading the Bible Leader's Guide
Drama, Skits, & Sketches (Ideas Library)
Drama, Skits, & Sketches 2 (Ideas Library)
Dramatic Pauses
Everyday Object Lessons
Games (Ideas Library)
Games 2 (Ideas Library)
Great Fundraising Ideas for Youth Groups
More Great Fundraising Ideas for Youth Groups
Great Retreats for Youth Groups
Holiday Ideas (Ideas Library)
Hot Illustrations for Youth Talks
More Hot Illustrations for Youth Talks
Still More Hot Illustrations for Youth Talks
Ideas Library on CD-ROM
Incredible Questionnaires for Youth Ministry
Junior High Game Nights
More Junior High Game Nights
Kickstarters: 101 Ingenious Intros to Just about Any Bible Lesson
Live the Life! Student Evangelism Training Kit
Memory Makers
The Next Level Leader's Guide

Play It! Great Games for Groups
Play It Again! More Great Games for Groups
Special Events (Ideas Library)
Spontaneous Melodramas
Student Leadership Training Manual
Super Sketches for Youth Ministry
Teaching the Bible Creatively
Videos That Teach
What Would Jesus Do? Youth Leader's Kit
Wild Truth Bible Lessons
Wild Truth Bible Lessons 2
Wild Truth Bible Lessons—Pictures of God
Worship Services for Youth Groups

DISCUSSION STARTERS

Discussion & Lesson Starters (Ideas Library)
Discussion & Lesson Starters 2 (Ideas Library)
Get 'Em Talking
Keep 'Em Talking!
High School TalkSheets
More High School TalkSheets
High School TalkSheets: Psalms and Proverbs
Junior High TalkSheets
More Junior High TalkSheets
Junior High TalkSheets: Psalms and Proverbs
Unfinished Sentences: 450 Tantalizing Statement-Starters to Get Teenagers Talking & Thinking
What If...? 450 Thought-Provoking Questions to Get Teenagers Talking, Laughing, and Thinking
Would You Rather...? 465 Provocative Questions to Get Teenagers Talking
Have You Ever...? 450 Intriguing Questions Guaranteed to Get Teenagers Talking

CLIP ART

ArtSource: Stark Raving Clip Art (print)
ArtSource: Youth Group Activities (print)
ArtSource CD-ROM: Clip Art Library Version 2.0

VIDEOS

EdgeTV
The Heart of Youth Ministry: A Morning with Mike Yaconelli
Purpose-Driven Youth Ministry Video Curriculum
Understanding Your Teenager Video Curriculum

STUDENT BOOKS

Downloading the Bible: A Rough Guide to the New Testament
Downloading the Bible: A Rough Guide to the Old Testament
Grow For It Journal
Grow For It Journal through the Scriptures
Spiritual Challenge Journal: The Next Level
Teen Devotional Bible
What Would Jesus Do? Spiritual Challenge Journal
Wild Truth Journal for Junior Highers
Wild Truth Journal—Pictures of God